TOUGH TRUCKS

CHEVROLET SILVERADO

BY LARRY MACK

TORQUE™

BELLWETHER MEDIA • MINNEAPOLIS, MN

Are you ready to take it to the extreme? Torque books thrust you into the action-packed world of sports, vehicles, mystery, and adventure. These books may include dirt, smoke, fire, and dangerous stunts.
WARNING read at your own risk.

This edition first published in 2019 by Bellwether Media, Inc.

Library of Congress Cataloging-in-Publication Data

Names: Mack, Larry, author.
Title: Chevrolet Silverado / by Larry Mack.
Description: Minneapolis, MN : Bellwether Media, Inc., 2019. | Series: Torque. Tough Trucks | Includes bibliographical references and index. | Audience: Ages 7-12.
Identifiers: LCCN 2018001844 (print) | LCCN 2018012086 (ebook) | ISBN 9781626178915 (hardcover : alk. paper) | ISBN 9781681036106 (ebook)
Subjects: LCSH: Silverado truck–Juvenile literature. | Chevrolet trucks–Juvenile literature. | CYAC: Trucks. | LCGFT: Picture books. | Instructional and educational works.
Classification: LCC TL230.5.S454 (ebook) | LCC TL230.5.S454 M33 2019 (print) | DDC 629.223/2-dc23
LC record available at https://lccn.loc.gov/2018001844

Editor: Betsy Rathburn Designer: Josh Brink

Printed in the United States of America, North Mankato, MN.

TABLE OF CONTENTS

THE CHEVROLET SILVERADO AT WORK

The building site buzzes with excitement. Workers hurry to complete the project. It must be done before the day ends!

The workday is almost over. But there is one last job to be done. A trailer needs to be moved. This job needs a powerful truck.

DEERE
DEERE

One worker has an idea. She climbs into the **cab** of a Chevrolet Silverado. She backs up until the truck is parked in front of the trailer.

Her coworkers attach the trailer to the Silverado's **hitch**. She fires up the pickup and pulls the trailer away. The Chevrolet Silverado was the perfect truck for the job!

CHEVROLET SILVERADO HISTORY

Before there were Chevrolet trucks, there were Chevrolet cars. In 1911, a Swiss race car driver named Louis Chevrolet decided to build cars.

Louis partnered with William C. Durant to create a new company. They named it Chevrolet. People liked Chevrolet so much that the company earned the Chevy nickname. Chevy cars were a hit!

Louis Chevrolet

THE BOWTIE

CHEVY'S FAMOUS LOGO LOOKS LIKE A BOWTIE! SOME PEOPLE SAY WILLIAM DURANT COPIED IT FROM THE DESIGN HE SAW ON HOTEL WALLPAPER. OTHERS SAY HE GOT IT FROM A NEWSPAPER AD!

William C. Durant

Chevy worked hard on new truck designs, too. They introduced their first truck in 1918. Then in 1960, Chevy introduced the Chevrolet C/K. These trucks would become some of the world's most popular pickups!

1966 Chevrolet C/K

CHEVY C/K

CHEVY C/K PICKUPS ENJOYED FOUR DECADES OF SUCCESS. C MODELS HAD TWO-WHEEL DRIVE. K MODELS CAME WITH FOUR-WHEEL DRIVE.

1999 Chevrolet Silverado

But the best Chevy trucks were still to come. In 1999, the company replaced the C/K with the Silverado. It was named the 1999 Truck of the Year!

CHEVROLET SILVERADO TODAY

Today, the most powerful Silverados can pull more than 10,000 pounds (4,536 kilograms). They have **payloads** of over 5,000 pounds (2,268 kilograms)!

Other features make hauling easy for the Silverado, too. The truck has **sensors** to tell drivers when their trailer is swaying too much. Other sensors stop the truck from rolling backwards on steep hills.

FEATURES AND TECHNOLOGY

Chevrolet Silverado High Country

The Chevrolet Silverado comes in many styles. Trucks with regular cabs carry two people. Crew cabs have backseats. They can carry even more passengers!

The truck's body has some features that make it more **fuel-efficient**. For example, a **spoiler** on the **tailgate** cuts down **drag**. This helps the Silverado use less fuel!

Chevrolet Silverado Trailboss

Some Silverados come with **four-wheel drive**. Four-wheel drive helps wheels grip the ground more easily. It helps drivers cross rough **terrain**.

SPECIAL EDITION

THE SPECIAL OPS SILVERADO HAS TINTED WINDOWS, BLACK WHEELS, AND TOUGH TIRES. MONEY RAISED BY THE SPECIAL OPS EDITION GOES TO THE NAVY SEAL MUSEUM.

Some features keep drivers safe. For example, Teen Driver Mode is for young drivers. It warns if they are driving too fast. It even shuts off the radio if someone is not wearing a seatbelt!

Inside the cab, a Silverado has comfortable seats with lots of legroom. In some **models**, an extra-large cab offers even more space.

Electronic gadgets help passengers stay comfortable and safe. A touch screen helps drivers **navigate** and back up more easily. One feature warns the driver if they are too close to another car!

2018 CHEVROLET SILVERADO 3500HD SPECIFICATIONS

ENGINE	6.0L V8 ENGINE
HORSEPOWER	360 HP (268 KILOWATTS) @ 5,400 RPM
TORQUE	380 LB-FT (53 KG-M) @ 4,200 RPM
TOWING CAPACITY	14,600 POUNDS (6,620 KILOGRAMS)
MAXIMUM PAYLOAD	5,671 POUNDS (2,572 KILOGRAMS)
FUEL ECONOMY	ABOUT 16 MILES PER GALLON
CURB WEIGHT	7,239 POUNDS (3,284 KILOGRAMS)
WHEEL SIZE	18 INCHES (46 CENTIMETERS)

TRUCK OF THE FUTURE

Drivers love the Silverado for its strength and power. It is one of the most popular trucks in the United States.

The Silverado will only get better. The company is already introducing trucks for coming model years. In the future, the Chevy Silverado will be even more powerful!

HOW TO SPOT A CHEVROLET SILVERADO

BOWTIE LOGO

TAILGATE SPOILER

RECTANGULAR GRILLE

GLOSSARY

cab—the area of a pickup where the driver and passengers sit

drag—a force that slows down the motion of a truck

four-wheel drive—a feature that allows the engine to turn all four of a vehicle's wheels at once

fuel-efficient—able to use less fuel

hitch—the part of a truck that connects to a trailer

models—specific kinds of trucks

navigate—to use maps and directions to get around

payloads—the total amounts of weight trucks can haul in their cabs and boxes

sensors—devices that help a truck know what other objects are nearby

spoiler—a part on the back of a truck that helps the truck grip the road

tailgate—a gate at the back of a truck that can be let down

terrain—the surface of an area of land

TO LEARN MORE

AT THE LIBRARY

Bowman, Chris. *Pickup Trucks.* Minneapolis, Minn.: Bellwether Media, 2018.

Mack, Larry. *Ford F-150.* Minneapolis, Minn.: Bellwether Media, 2019.

Mack, Larry. *Ram 1500.* Minneapolis, Minn.: Bellwether Media, 2019.

ON THE WEB

Learning more about the Chevrolet Silverado is as easy as 1, 2, 3.

1. Go to www.factsurfer.com.

2. Enter "Chevrolet Silverado" into the search box.

3. Click the "Surf" button and you will see a list of related web sites.

With factsurfer.com, finding more information is just a click away.

INDEX

The images in this book are reproduced through the courtesy of: RL GNZLZ/ Flickr, front cover (hero); Andrey Kuzmin, front cover (title texture), pp. 9 (metal), 10 (metal), 17 (metal), 19 (metal); Vadim Bochkarev, front cover (background); xpixe, front cover (top mud, bottom mud); diogoppr, front cover (mud splash); Jeramey Lende, pp. 2-3 (logo), 9 (logo); betto rodrigues, pp. 2-3 (truck); Yulia Plekhanova, pp. 2-3 (background); Chevrolet, pp. 4-5, 6-7, 12-13, 14-15, 16-17, 17 (truck), 18-19, 19 (truck), 20-21, 21 (right); CSU Archive/ AgeFotostock, p. 8; Wikipedia, pp. 8-9; Matthew Richardson/ Alamy, p. 10, Lord Laitinen, pp. 10-11, sociologas, p. 21 (metal); Ed Aldridge, p. 21 (left, middle).